GERMANY

Also by Caroline Finkelstein

Windows Facing East

GERMANY

Caroline Finkelstein

Carnegie Mellon University Press
Pittsburgh 1995

Acknowledgments

Grateful acknowledgement is made to the following periodicals in which these poems first appeared:

The American Poetry Review: "The Brave Little Tailleurs Of 1935," "The Modes Of Our Most Perfect Lady"
Harvard Magazine: "The Firefighter," "Honesty," "Vanitas"
The Massachusetts Review: "The Gods"
Poetry: "For That Husband," "Not Responsible," "The Soul In The Bowl," "With Fox Eyes," "Vacation"
Tikkun: "Anger"
TriQuarterly: "The Dwelling"
Seneca Review: "Thanksgiving," "A Round With Envy"
Sojourner: "Casus Belli," "Persephone's Notes," "Deutsch"
Virginia Quarterly Review: "Autumn Again," "See The Pyramids," "The Lovers"
Willow Springs: "1950," "The Rescue"
Witness: "Exhaustion," "Our Tale From Hoffmann," "Shabby Private Club"

I wish to offer deepest thanks to Robert Clinton, Donald Hall, Louis Asekoff, Jane Kenyon, Ellen Bryant Voigt and Nicholas Finkelstein.

My thanks also to the MacDowell Colony.

The publication of this book is supported by grants from the National Endowment for the Arts in Washington, D.C., a Federal agency, and from the Pennsylvania Council on the Arts.

Contents

III

IV

For Gabriel

"Spring returned to Badenheim."

—Aharon Appelfeld

I

BRINK

This is the hinterland, quiet and idle.
Trees and the river. River and farms.
In the courtyard in the leafy shade, we see
only minor officials, and on tranquil evenings
people drinking coffee on the porches of their houses.
These are the provinces. Every now and then
we hear an animal cry out, not loud.

But the night is mightier than the separate voices
of the creatures. The night throws silence
over geese floating on the lake
and the visible, variable stars. The lamps are lit
when we walk out; when we return
we see the sturdy servant girl
handling the heaviest valises. There are many travelers.

It is August and the days are thick.
Wagons are driven to the tavern
and the tavernkeeper, sad and standing in the doorway,
what is he thinking? Shame is a mood here. Now
the already migrating birds hover
near an orchard where some drunken men
will soon make the doctor busy.

What is the soul for? Whither have we come?
We no longer ask. Here a field is a field,
and canopies of shadow endure without philosophy.
That man trembling as he waits,
clearly he is anxious. But can't he read
the schedule? There are so many
local trains, so many stations in the birches.

THE BRAVE LITTLE TAILLEURS OF 1935

For madame, the would-be prince's
silk-shot pretty, we make outerwear
to imitate the silver money of the moon;
we make the garments ripple, shape
peignoirs out of heaven's
drapery; the world is on the bias.
Madame is up for lunch? Turn, oh sloe-
eyed fantasy of berries under cream,
we need to cut you, hem you into mirrors
where's there's safety: only
your reflection. Is madame ingesting
tabloids, news reeling like a tango
as flies crawl across a dusty bowl?
Never mind, madame, we will fix and fix.

Wonder is the ice we stitch unmelting
in your bodice. Wonder
is the spangled glory
on a number for a little evening
slumming. Slow and ghostly
moves the satin train
from your shoulder's pale milk.

And the bangled, never freckled wrists of you
like willow shoots that wave away
a humid air, an odor . . .
And the jingle of the phone when you are wired
hordes of China roses piled high as lobster
salad. Within those aspic jewels
real pearls suspend like packs of spores.
And your favorite girls, the big dog
that they bring to you, the laughter . . .

For madame, the slimmest
figure on the esplanade, we build
wedding cakes of lace for lying down
and lying in.
You've recovered from the baby? Look,
we've sewn a sacque for it with yellow stars.

OUR TALE FROM HOFFMANN

The women are one pretty corpse after another,
and the men, gifted
with mortuary obsessions,
delicately tailored vagabonds wandering
the borders of ecstasy: the little girl
dies when she sings, sings when she dies —

and the somnambulistic daughter
and the father like the rest of us but more
restless and naked
are the imps, gruesome
supernaturals from the hunting lodges.

They arrive on chilly nights, worshipping
the marriage of disease with creativity —
and we never tell them: *go*. They are so lonely and old.

VANITAS

A great cathedral city.
Dark cloud over rose window over high Gothic door.
In the distance: the *earth*works?
In the foreground: cobbles.
A wagon loaded with household effects.

The Holy Infant. The Holy Infant and Mother.
Herring, firewood, iodine, coffee.
A horse on the left, horse piss.

White: hands, linen, light, aspirin.
Black: lingerie, telephone, mascara, a greatcoat
in the bedroom, a rolled-down window shade.
Cigarettes on the rim of the sink.

In the snow, when it snows, the ragged types.
(In the snow, when it snows, provocateurs.)

Sounds: metaphysics and electric wires.
Sounds: the frontier: rumbling.
Professions: butchering.

Faith in God and justice, human and Divine.
The very apparent rib-cage of that horse.
Tallow, garlic, manna, soldier, chess.

Stars! Vega, Deneb, Rigel in the constellation of Orion,
the enormous star of David, and the North star.

A switchman, a brakeman, the butcher a baker.

From memory: *on an embankment, very early summer,*
a whole swath of the most exquisite violets, violet blue
of course, but also white so finely lined with blue
and overhead as many larks, it seemed, as flowers.

A photograph of a small boy in a sweater on a sofa.
In a minute's time a picture of his wedding.
Then divorce; then her legal marriage to a fairer man.

Many widows in the recent photos. Many golden watch chains,
much pomaded hair, hat pins, velvet collars, veils,
black dresses, underwear and gloves and calfskin shoes.

Platform of the station. Clock within the steeple.
Wooden trunks, trunks of wicker, baggage rack,
a brown freight train, a long freight train.
A long blue river in the city. And Mr. Medieval,
scythe in hand, a terrible thinness about him.

DEUTSCH

There is a male child on the stoop,
with a dream in his eyes

of yielding, lord, not yielding
to what is called slavery —

he waits there in his brown shoes
one summer and the next —

such is his portrait
with the dry leaves

already detaching

as his mother, fixed in the window's
inserts of light, labors to watch him

enter his life. In silence

the oak trees go crimson.
And huge, pathetic anger visits the world.

And darker red burns in the forest.

THE GODS

for Mariève

We were so weird when we were kids
there was a war.

Butchers practiced medicine.
Fairies had no wings.

Feed me a bottle, baby, sweetheart,
cried our Mama doll but we were birds

sitting in the coat-tree shade
with the invisible and random

camera shutter clicking.

There was normal apparatus in the kitchen
but we were queer plus sleepy

and the oven had a window.
The sink was deep, a vat.

Potatoes grew white eyes.
And another thing: we couldn't stay awake.

So then the bombs would fall.

ANGER

Selma, a child not a child but a Jew
goes to the store for milk. This is Lodz
where rumor has the chickens plotting . . .

    In their necklaces of lice the chickens sway
and gabble at their prayers as if . . .
as if the holy Sabbath were a barnyard!

Soon. Soon. This is Lodz the dogs will eat.

SUCCOR

The darling, the big-eyed darling under quilts,
is so sick she's almost dead and then she is.
Her Papa kisses her dead eyes; her Mama
sheets the mirror. And Warsaw disappears.

But this is sentimental.

She survives the transport to the camp
but she's crazed by now and like a windmill on the ramp
so when they shoot her two times in the head
her feet beat a while on the gravel.

THE MODES OF OUR MOST PERFECT LADY

In the courtyard, in the long hallways,
I would glimpse them most deliberately
persisting in their roughneck lusts.
Their occasional quiet served to underscore
their real natures: in those pauses
I heard glass about to break.
It was a time of living wire. Some nights
they smashed the moon.

                                        But observe how I've conceived,
by God's hands and my wits,
life as it should be, fragrant and conducive
to imagination. And them?
They cough; they salivate in terror; they sweep the beach
like crabs.
When witnesses come upon this fate
I have them beaten into silence.
I need to have this silence; I need poetry.

LITTLE CITIZENS

look I say (they look) jump I say (they jump)
I hear them hear my hearing
I oversee their sleeping *close your eyes* (they do)

> *this is the shoe and this is the foot*
> *the shoe is to move go slow* I say *beware*
> this is an angel in the form of a cow

(I ease the abstractions)

then they are furtive and blurring my voice
then in my yard the birds argue like brothers
the blue jays and grey

I let them be the trees the wind begins to whine
and see them (intelligent) stand
stay I say give I say you will I say and (*yes* is dirt)

they root there swaying green and shadow

EXHAUSTION

The Divine sighed, cleared the table
and handed the tablecloth to the angel who did the laundry.
Another one swept; it had been a hard day.
And see how late it was: witness the children.

Why had no one calmed the children?

NOT RESPONSIBLE

The floodlights come on: look,
a Jewish girl without a permit for her bicycle
stands caught in Prague; it's 1938,
for the love of God!
Can't you do something?

Wait a minute. You're crazy;
that was fifty years ago; you weren't born;
turn the floodlights off,
go back to sleep, dream geese
carried under the arm of an old woman

walking in new shoes in 1938; she walks
in lavish twilight
toward a black mountain of shoes.

II

LEITMOTIV

"As I was ferried over the Rhine, I saw
one of the workers, an ugly girl, sweating
as she uncoiled heavy rope
                              and I grew excited

like in childhood
when women steered my life
and I imagined them tormented slaves.

That thinking never stopped.

The poor wretch before me,
and the river pierced with fish

were bodies anyone could notice, vivid, silent things

completely disappearing when I wrote,
there are no boundaries.

                    Also on board were Jews."

A ROMANTIC NATURE

"My parents darkened, darkened like silver
in the bright cold world of closing doors . . .
Regret and Longing fed me.

My mouth was full of the milky moon; my eyes,
when twilight chilled the woods
were terrified but thrilled.
                    Of the white roe
in the glade, I begged: *transfigure me.*

Then music played so sadly, recalling the impossible
and I felt magnetized, drawn
from my body to a song of long ago

when I was thrown down
by an undressed woman, that music on me, like teeth . . ."

PERSEPHONE'S NOTES

There is a shapeliness in grief

and in silence, in the snow, a remembered thunder
like a bee, like a ribbon in the youngest child's hair,

a booming and a recalled view
we call a meadow, flowers in the meadow.

So the world is full of formal nattering and rules,
music and the rule of random, consequence

and precincts.
Below this world is hell.

***

In hell I learned the uses for the body.
Underneath: *like this*.

And I was in it voiceless.
Then a total grey, the hell of huge indifference.

***

That there never is a moral.
That black birds gather in wet meadows

early in the spring and peal
like metal and with cherries on their wings.

I want to because I do, he said, *beautiful, I want to.*

SHABBY PRIVATE CLUB

Not for a moment have I forgotten that dark laundry.
Two blocks east of the Hudson the tub was filled with it.
When they needed to infinitely wash the child
the clock of the universe hung like a moon in the kitchen
fronting the nine-stories-down avenue. You couldn't jump out,
it was bath-time noon & night.
We are at war, said Daddy. Damp clothes ticked on the tiles.

A dream entered me in florid silence like a body
upside down, like Mussolini
swinging in the movies, black & white,
& Mother was beside me with chocolate cherries in her hands.
She was dizzy, too, & peerless on her platform
shoes. Dead fish slept in the fish-store window
& someone left the oven on,
someone left the oven on
& someone put gauze across the light bulb
so it was never night & never day
& every day
people coughed exhaustedly in sheds
as the rituals grew limitless & control abandoned —

Not for a moment have I forgotten those brown, wet shirts.

CASUS BELLI

Miss third-person-singular-about-to-be-devoured, she's
the girl walking into randomness, the girl watching the girl

walking into randomness, walking into dangers.
They're giving her shoes because she's the girl

walking toward a swaying; they're giving her dark eyes,
giving her light hair, a blouse with buttons, jeans and a flower

(they always give a flower). They're giving her a landscape of
field and sidewalk, exurb and mall, and bushes

burning in summer; they're teaching her to count
lice on the minotaur's back, and screams

of birds in the air —
She's walking in the wind and she has a coat;

they've given that to her; they say:
a nice navy blue wool coat; look how pretty

she is in it, what a cut,
how very shapely, how unusual —

They want to say *unusual* and say it really often;
they practice at the vanity; in the bathroom steam

they slowly form the words: *how un-u-zhu-al.*
They form the vowels behind their teeth.

She's watching smoke do tricks in the steam; it's
the breath of a trembling bull like spume off the water in fog;

she's watching; she's swaying; they say
they have pills for the swaying. For walking

they've given her shoes, unusual shoes,
unusual girl, Miss Archetype-neophyte-lady-of-

sorrow, neophyte queen of the spring, unusual mouth
their hands clamp down on, their very justified hands —

THE BOND

We went down to the mines, my brother and I,
but there were no mines; if there had been mines
they were gone long ago, and the songs
of the mines: also gone;
what had sent us was rumor. We went home
to the author of rumor. She said,
how was it down at the mines?

My brother and I, we went over the stile
to the field where the sheep grazed
but there were no sheep and there was no grass.

Living in the house we listened for the sirens
and riding in the car we heard the war.
When we went in to dinner . . .

                              were we crazy?

My brother married over and over; he goes
down to the mines; he goes
to hunger and rumor. Sheep speak in the dark
but there are no sheep; there were never any sheep.
And there is no stile. I leap over the stile.

FOR THAT HUSBAND

Late at night and you thrashing
as if locked in your mother's dark,

the stillness is outside,
the stars are still

and I am still
the woman of your dream which means

it's terrible: you held in
banging at the oval of a bone

as one needing to be born
tries almost anything,

a wild rip of skin,
that push to break for air —

THE PRINCIPALS OF HOUSE
AND GARDEN: ADAM AND EVE

They went on about the *vista*.

They went on about the vista and elements and words in a series
and all the while as the poor solemn ruth in them arranged the
furniture,

they trembled; endowed with an animal eye and ear they trembled
on the loam of the carpet, in corridors and pathways.

Ten red fingernails, the image of a woman's hands,
distracted them from their purposes and likewise the new lettuce

draining on the drainboards of the world,

God! a whole kitchen could have hidden what they liked to do for
years
before they went upstairs to darkness and the jury.

Centuries passed (you've heard about this?)
and while the two faces and their accumulating cries and the
leafyness

and painterly attitudes and those small brown hairs
held and held, they passed in and out of their clay bodies

taking other names: *iris, yellow archangel.*

THE LOVERS

Here they are, a voice says.
Like alabaster, the two figures.

The bed, the sleeping and the meadow, says a voice,
and the meaning the two of them can't locate.

Any minute now they find it?

The man and the woman who are here inside a voice
that would love to sing efficiently.

Here they are as still-lifes getting into days of objects.

Dear secret, imagine them the way you want them, imagine
them transforming one another.

Poor mice, although they aren't that.
Poor Saturdays of rain.

***

Any minute now and hand-in-hand they will discover
the small meaning.

Just as soon as they are finished, dear instigator god of exile,

lingering and exile, dear myth of charity,
god-the-irretrievable, any minute now

it will be completely over

and the room they are spinning in together, ask it
does it breathe, is it dizzy?

***

38

And their upraised faces, and their legs, how badly they want
anxiety, dear modern context,

oh the hummingbirded pace of them,
this crazy-to-make-an-angel pair, cut and pasted

as if they were the upper air's *vocation*, a notion
of accretion-by-accretion form

blown full of breath.

These hurried bodies and their languor, dear invisible design.
And the meaning never located. And that poor voice speaking.

Promise you won't leave.

GERMANY

It was a church, our being with one another.
The spire and the apse, symbols
for a man and woman,
were of stone and smooth and grey.
There is nothing tepid in a stone.

Rain engraved itself upon the spire; wine
spilled on the altar; this was life
full of mishap and puzzling
circumstance.

               Outside, the human images
carried market baskets through the square
as the lovely willows yellowed
year after mortal year.

But we were beyond these
odors of candlesmoke and flowers;
we were a church: death kept us occupied.
And if not death then the sanctity of affliction.

III

A ROUND WITH ENVY

She was saying *wounded* like she was the monarch of it,

she was talking such delicate blue you could see
the depth of her bruise, with her bed in it,

and her waiters, hot as bonfires, fainting . . .
She was wearing white iris and sex, the natural world

with a tortoise-shell comb in its hand: and Christ!
if she commanded with dancing and dying again and forever

in the black dress, wasn't she gorgeous
and in terrible pain like the moon she invented,

like the bits of the sea she would feed you,
littlenecks in a broth.

Face it, wasn't she all that you wished for
yourself, describing the knife going in

so that everyone screamed, not with horror, but with absolute
passion, and then she was under the covers of childhood naked.

Just once, you would die for that life.

So your poems reappear. And a touch away is everything.

1950

The Austrian emperor shapes my life, shouting
come up, come in, to the American roller skater I am
on the West End Avenue of sycamores and UPS trucks and blinking
intensely nervous former Displaced Persons.
It is not a drowsy time, all the trees restlessly move
in Riverside Park where it is forbidden and excellent to roller skate
and where some men fish the Hudson, and some men, subjects,
look at the alien horizon which *is* . . . yet is impossible.

I am nine in the four rooms on the ninth floor
where we repeatedly dress, undress and bathe to Chopin etudes,
and down in the street there is so much brick architecture
and in the apartment so many cabbage roses on the walls,
also coffee and, of course, pigeons seen
on the side-street rooftops, always pigeons, sooty echoes
of the Empire's huge black eagles.

I skate after school; it is four o'clock on any afternoon
of traffic and slight shadows and the tailor on the corner;
these are small, sober hours where I move and I stand still.
I have no name for the passion in the air like smoke
and the defenselessness (don't stare)
of the human traffic and the repetition of pledges of allegiance
left and right and the spies, spies everywhere . . .

HONESTY

after a painting by Lucian Freud

Physical sadness: the child is too still
in the emptying room; the door shuts
too cautiously, as if an adult were closing it
and leaving, going out
into the street, into daytime, ordinary noon
where people walk
and it is Sunday there, not raining . . .

Nor is it

(is it?) in any way extraordinary
for the child to appear and reappear unmoving . . .

The shade sways and the light exposes
nothing excessively
twisted, just a table, window,
bed. Why lie about it? (Lie about it.)

MY PART IN THE SISTERHOOD

The latest post-teen odalisque
oddball wackadoo — my son's
her boyfriend, rebel graduate
schoolboy deploring the kinks of academe
but he's *at* it, at school
while she's nervous in Berlin,
rangy, underfed . . .

                              I had
a long, green, drop-dead dress
doing nothing in the closet
so I sent it overseas
to the blue little shoe
of a girl near the Wall who can't
buckle down, and I couldn't either.
I sent her a note: *wear it someplace.*

I didn't say: sad girl,
I've been inside the story
where the male model of the entire Nazi party
will not fuck his girlfriend
only slowly
eats some grapes and puts the grapeskins
one by one
across her naked belly . . .

SEE THE PYRAMIDS

Here's what's happening: everything. As the yews move,
as the ragged cedars flutter, and the Tigris and the
                                    Rappahannock flow,
here's my grandmother marketing a long way from Danzig.
She's already moved to Brooklyn; here's the bridge
and Mr. Whitman and isn't it a warm day? And what a blue sky
Picasso saunters under in the summers following the liberation,
and it's my grandmother again; here's her heart condition and
also ibis, wading ibis. Now my grandmother does her laundry,
singing, *see the pyramids along the Nile,* and weaving like a praying
Arab, and isn't that God checking out His green reflection
in the glass of Lever House and Pollack splashing rain
on canvas? How the palm fronds sway utterly
as the the old lady keeps singing, *you belong to me!*
Next, a flowering pear tree happens. Everyone: drink your tea.

VACATION

1.

Early summer and the beautiful babies are home,
their beautiful lips move, their arms swing in the sunlight.
Gold days and green. The grass and the aimless
parents in their chairs on the grass, and the birds
singing the sun up and down.
Moths go flying. Cool streams wander.

2.

It was a household much in love with music.
She opened the door and saw her shadow.
She didn't interfere. The trees and the moon — they didn't
interfere. The dog wanted to but the cat did not.
The beautiful baby was sleeping and sleeping.
Brahms sighed. She closed the door hard.

3.

How like an earnest world: the pink geranium!
No drama in the flower's petals, only sturdiness,
only faithful months of blooming. Yes,
justice is invisible in modern kingdoms
full of precious stones and boredom.
When you think of it, you order coffee. Calmly.

4.

I combed my child's hair, o dragonfly.
First it was a busy morning and then
the dusk came on all day.
It became solitary so quickly;
I walked through the air into a lonely body.
But there were seasonal variations: ferns, rain, no rain.

AUTUMN AGAIN

The bread of the world, sex, oh, trouble, trouble.

Fingers and teeth at the refectory table. Since dawn
the roil of it, one body and one body's hunger, multiplied, carried,

and the old paintings on the walls, always those
gardens of blame: *your honor, your worship, it was her.*

She is the art and the aftermath. And you swear
even the trees are exhausted by it, why else are they dying,

why else do the words, *rich woman,* ring like metal clanging?

She who has power over you . . .

It is a dark morning now. As if a tablecloth covered the sun,
as if the clouds were contempt only, blotching the light,

as if it didn't happen that by the billions the mother
holds her child's hand as he tells some particle of his day to her

and she listens while also (silently) singing a song that goes,
little-nape-of-the-neck, dearest-little-wide-brow, and is exultant,

exultant . . .

The loaves are baked.
Brown leaves and gold leaves fall to the grass.

THE SOUL IN THE BOWL

In the clay, in the grey
cool slip of the bed
of the creek, in a marriage
of water and matter,
it was formless —

in the night of it,
in the cornflowered
dawn of its being
asleep, it was whole
and alone —

like shadow, like ivy
climbing up slowly
in dreams, it flourished,
a star in the dark —

but the potter's empty hands
wrung with discontent
and the hard burning kiln
wanted
something to anneal —

when I look into my child's
face, I see
fine lines like writing
and like fracture.

OUTSIDE IN

For Adam

After the snake, the glass heart
in the eye of glass that watches,
after that *poise*, so beautiful on the ledge

in the snake's body, waiting —

the farmer is there in the patience and minerals,
in the deepening velvets dividing to multiply: leaves,
leaves and fruit in the long lanes

ploughed and harrowed smooth, and all summer

in the dominion of summer and shadow,
in the swaying and thickness
and roundness and dust and rain,

he bargains in the thriving: wheelbarrow
songtracks in the hot, dark dirt, the satin
meat of the tomatoes, and his breath in and out

like wind the next morning and the next morning after that.

OLD IMAGES

They study and do not wake
estranged: Abraham
      argues with his God; Isaac walks
                            uphill.

             Chicory blooms
the brief Polish summers
  blue like sky, like the undersides
of angel's wings.

          This is innocence
subdued. In the Midrash,

              a poor Jew is a white horse
wearing a red bridle.

IV

WITH FOX EYES

they were beasts it was wrong to call them that
it was wrong they weren't beasts
under the guiltless moon the sky a planetary blue

someone said God made us God was lonely
someone got a confirmation *do it now*

the weather was lousy in New York
in Berlin Nanking Rio someone swallowed whiskey
while the convoys idled leaking oil

then the shaky trains bled and there was crazy surgery
but the lindens anyway bloomed the chromy marigolds

and goldenrod

I was a child I went inside a box
I was a wild fox mouth eating currants
in the doorways I stood watching with my fox eyes

here are the tragic dresses shoes photos the Imari
here are memory and body growing older

it was wrong to call them beasts they weren't beasts
because beasts are what the gods would be
without despair within on fire

THE GIRL GHOST IN HER PETTICOAT

That characteristic rustling you hear
is tafetta, paper taffeta.
There is about to be a dance; December snow
is a lightweight curtain on the building.

And the passersby hurrying to abstraction —
who knows what they think?

The ghost, it isn't her moment; it isn't
really her life, only borrowed pieces: grosgrain
ribbon, French ribbon,
sufferings chiefly from other sources,

not that there isn't a wound —

What you see is: dusk and expectation,
the very tissue of her body,
                    and all of it beyond her —

No voice, blue dress, blue dress.

THANKSGIVING

And sunlight compliments the figures
usually in the dark; plainly now

they want an atmosphere
of white damask and brocade,

white and yellow spider mums —

and the woman's red fingernails
for once in kindness

touching the man's neck
while straightening his tie,

and the man perishing with desire
in the illuminated rooms and mirrors —

                                       is it too cruel
to describe them as they are: alive

solely in the book of fury
that is my consciousness?

Those ignited oak leaves
reluctant to let go.

And the heavy, laden table.

CONFLICT WITHIN

In the sunshine what an argument you made
against returning. What a bright day it was,

the white, the yellow flowers.

There was nothing in your gestures to misinterpret,
no gauzy arc of arm, or a smile not a smile,

when you spoke your voice took up the foreground.

To go back, you said, was awful.

Where you stood, straight as the spiked grass,
it must have been just noon because I can't remember shadows

and I can't remember foaming thickets brimming over
but the weeds in that light looked huge.

Pull them out, you said, impatient but not unkind
and then knelt down yourself.

Forsythia bloomed behind you and overhead the sky

showed blue continuous air
complementing all the edges of the world.

Those many fields and houses.
But I wanted to return, I wanted to amend.

How brilliant it appeared. And you, so full of virtue.

CAMP GREYLOCK

Remembered ten-year olds,
bodies and wings
in this page's white,

they wander into
the archery field
behind "Chippewa"

naming their business: girlhood;
meanwhile it is
July, exactly mid-

green in the dream
they have: a sudden rendezvous
of rain and lake: the rain

piercing the lake sucking
the rain. What a narrative
they are, dawdling toward

swimming lessons
at their address in the hills —
such sister clusters: lilies.

THE DWELLING

So many times I offered my house, painted the big walls white
for you and set out bowls where Oriental birds showed

in the concavities. I gave you long halls of wide boards
and the windows, doors, and the height of the rooms were more

invitations:
come in, observe, sit still; even disapprove if you have to.

And in the bedroom, so many times,
I was sure you didn't hear me because I couldn't read your looks

but listen, I was like that then, even the dog resting on the rug
worried me; maybe he was a sick dog.

I wanted you to like the roses.
Finally, I loved you. In the humid air of late summer, it wasn't easy.

You lay next to me asleep and I hated you asleep
and I hated your silent, withheld body.

Then I walked toward the garden dreaming invisible hands
weeding the perfect gravel paths you made and I see now

how we abetted one another, forcing beauty to control
imagination. I am no longer young.

Something releases the wind that flickers the lights.
The walls begin to fail and cool air enters. Can you see me?

HIGH FALL

I was watching you I was not crying
for once your need to be solitary
wasn't my agenda my daily reminder the moon

the firefly destruction the leaves blowing began
and the herons the numerous geese
circled the pond the pine tops the field our garden

I wasn't crying in it I wasn't going freaky
blaming you for the perpetual
lady of losses

the end of the story wasn't the point
of the story burnt gold spelled
in the wet yellow leaves

I wanted to but didn't have to
tell you that I saw you
help yourself up beautifully privately

everywhere I saw the rust the copper beeches
the pear trees haze of wasps
the light grey paper nests the light grey paper sky

and the glittering in the rain

NIGHTMARE

There is a question right now entering
that place already too familiar

where it is just the naked two of them
in the now-and-again fierce rain

and there isn't any killing, only enormous cleanliness,
lilac but no memory of lilac in the blue air they breathe.

And any minute now he'll ask,
what in hell have you done?

With his hands on his hips, desiring.

GERMANY: REPRISE

The man who loves me hates me.
I know this to be the essence
of passion: the brilliant sun
under which the grass is burning,
and I come from a family in flames —

Sometimes walking in the beech grove
we find a thrush's egg fallen from the nest
and I tell you it throbs with blue,
the tiny thing feels like a blow in the face,
it is so beautiful —

And sometimes when it snows,
iron doves fasten us down in the whirling
ashes and shadows.

THE RESCUE

A vast dust came upon them inside what they called a marriage.

Laughing their metal laughs.

Birds and the dog on rubble called the lawn.

I knew a panic clanged in him when he saw her body threatening
his erasure; I knew her at the edge of what she called the page,

every day stricken there, tugged
to the bottom of a lake

and the Old World deer feeding at its shore
as the sun hustled morning out (come *on*) and over

hemlocks and the Interstate.
What they called history also fell as dust, and someone

playing tenor sax all through the Second War
was seen as grit fallen on the mantel and it wasn't wrong

to hear a small, sweet orchestra begin
swinging, swaying, saying, *look, look, look, look,*

to the girl singer in the light —
until it was blue dawn: what they called the break of day.

They saw themselves as particles in rain, delay, the dust,

numbered, undefined and vague.

And how did I enhance their lines? With beauty, with cruelty.

NOTE

The story referred to in "My Part In The Sisterhood" is from *The Gastronomical Me* by M.F.K. Fisher, and the chapter that contains it is called "To Feed Such Hunger."

Carnegie Mellon Poetry

1975
The Living and the Dead, Ann Hayes
In the Face of Descent, T. Alan Broughton

1976
The Week the Dirigible Came, Jay Meek
Full of Lust and Good Usage, Stephen Dunn

1977
How I Escaped from the Labyrinth and Other Poems, Philip Dacey
The Lady from the Dark Green Hills, Jim Hall
For Luck: Poems 1962-1977, H. L. Van Brunt
By the Wreckmaster's Cottage, Paula Rankin

1978
New & Selected Poems, James Bertolino
The Sun Fetcher, Michael Dennis Browne
A Circus of Needs, Stephen Dunn
The Crowd Inside, Elizabeth Libbey

1979
Paying Back the Sea, Philip Dow
Swimmer in the Rain, Robert Wallace
Far from Home, T. Alan Broughton
The Room Where Summer Ends, Peter Cooley
No Ordinary World, Mekeel McBride

1980
And the Man Who Was Traveling Never Got Home, H. L. Van Brunt
Drawing on the Walls, Jay Meek
The Yellow House on the Corner, Rita Dove
The 8-Step Grapevine, Dara Wier
The Mating Reflex, Jim Hall

1981
A Little Faith, John Skoyles
Augers, Paula Rankin
Walking Home from the Icehouse, Vern Rutsala
Work and Love, Stephen Dunn
The Rote Walker, Mark Jarman
Morocco Journal, Richard Harteis
Songs of a Returning Soul, Elizabeth Libbey

1982
The Granary, Kim R. Stafford
Calling the Dead, C. G. Hanzlicek
Dreams Before Sleep, T. Alan Broughton
Sorting It Out, Anne S. Perlman
Love Is Not a Consolation; It Is a Light, Primus St. John

1983
The Going Under of the Evening Land, Mekeel McBride
Museum, Rita Dove
Air and Salt, Eve Shelnutt
Nightseasons, Peter Cooley

1984
Falling from Stardom, Jonathan Holden
Miracle Mile, Ed Ochester
Girlfriends and Wives, Robert Wallace
Earthly Purposes, Jay Meek
Not Dancing, Stephen Dunn
The Man in the Middle, Gregory Djanikian
A Heart Out of This World, David James
All You Have in Common, Dara Wier

1985
Smoke from the Fires, Michael Dennis Browne
Full of Lust and Good Usage, Stephen Dunn (2nd edition)
Far and Away, Mark Jarman
Anniversary of the Air, Michael Waters
To the House Ghost, Paula Rankin
Midwinter Transport, Anne Bromley

1986
Seals in the Inner Harbor, Brendan Galvin
Thomas and Beulah, Rita Dove
Further Adventures With You, C. D. Wright
Fifteen to Infinity, Ruth Fainlight
False Statements, Jim Hall
When There Are No Secrets, C. G. Hanzlicek

1987
Some Gangster Pain, Gillian Conoley
Other Children, Lawrence Raab
Internal Geography, Richard Harteis
The Van Gogh Notebook, Peter Cooley
A Circus of Needs, Stephen Dunn (2nd edition)
Ruined Cities, Vern Rutsala
Places and Stories, Kim R. Stafford

1988

Preparing to Be Happy, T. Alan Broughton
Red Letter Days, Mekeel McBride
The Abandoned Country, Thomas Rabbitt
The Book of Knowledge, Dara Wier
Changing the Name to Ochester, Ed Ochester
Weaving the Sheets, Judith Root

1989

Recital in a Private Home, Eve Shelnutt
A Walled Garden, Michael Cuddihy
The Age of Krypton, Carol J. Pierman
Land That Wasn't Ours, David Keller
Stations, Jay Meek
The Common Summer: New and Selected Poems, Robert Wallace
The Burden Lifters, Michael Waters
Falling Deeply into America, Gregory Djanikian
Entry in an Unknown Hand, Franz Wright

1990

Why the River Disappears, Marcia Southwick
Staying Up For Love, Leslie Adrienne Miller
Dreamer, Primus St. John

1991

Permanent Change, John Skoyles
Clackamas, Gary Gildner
Tall Stranger, Gillian Conoley
The Gathering of My Name, Cornelius Eady
A Dog in the Lifeboat, Joyce Peseroff
Raised Underground, Renate Wood
Divorce: A Romance, Paula Rankin

1992

Modern Ocean, James Harms
The Astonished Hours, Peter Cooley
You Won't Remember This, Michael Dennis Browne
Twenty Colors, Elizabeth Kirschner
First A Long Hesitation, Eve Shelnutt
Bountiful, Michael Waters
Blue for the Plough, Dara Wier
All That Heat in a Cold Sky, Elizabeth Libbey

1993

Trumpeter, Jeannine Savard
Cuba, Ricardo Pau-Llosa
The Night World and the Word Night, Franz Wright
The Book of Complaints, Richard Katrovas

1994

If Winter Come: Collected Poems, 1967–1992, Alvin Aubert
Of Desire and Disorder, Wayne Dodd
Ungodliness, Leslie Adrienne Miller
Rain, Henry Carlile
Windows, Jay Meek
A Handful of Bees, Dzvinia Orlowsky

1995

Germany, Caroline Finkelstein
Housekeeping in a Dream, Laura Kasischke
About Distance, Gregory Djanikian
Wind of the White Dresses, Mekeel McBride
Above the Tree Line, Kathy Mangan
In the Country of Elegies, T. Alan Broughton
Scenes from the Light Years, Anne C. Bromley
Quartet, Angela Ball